Supported using public funding by
ARTS COUNCIL
ENGLAND

LOTTERY FUNDED

Front cover: Marcelino Sambé as Basilio and Yasmine Naghdi as Kitri in *Don Quixote* © 2019 ROH. Photograph by Andrej Uspenski

Back cover: artists of The Royal Ballet in *La Bayadère* © 2018 ROH. Photograph by Bill Cooper

Inside cover: Romany Pajdak, Leticia Dias, Kristen McNally, Ashley Dean, Gemma Pitchley-Gale and Mayara Magri in *The Concert* © 2018 ROH. Photograph by Alice Pennefather

First published in 2019 by the Royal Opera House
in association with Oberon Books Ltd
Oberon Books Ltd
521 Caledonian Road, London N7 9RH
Tel +44 (0)20 7607 3637
info@oberonbooks.com
www.oberonbooks.com

Compilation copyright © Royal Opera House 2019

Text copyright © Royal Opera House 2019

The Royal Opera House is hereby identified as
the author of this book in accordance with section
77 of the Copyright, Designs and Patents Act 1988.

Design: Konstantinos Vasdekis

For the Royal Opera House:

Picture Editor: Grace Allwood

Copy Editor: Jane Lawes

Every effort has been made to trace the copyright holders
of all images reprinted in this book. Acknowledgement is
made in all cases where the image source is available, but
we would be grateful for information about any images
where sources could not be traced.

A catalogue record for this book is available from the
British Library.

PB ISBN 9781786828064

Printed and bound
by CPI Group (UK) Ltd, Croydon, CR0 4YY.

Royal Opera House
Covent Garden
London WC2E 9DD
Box Office +44 (0)20 7304 4000
www.roh.org.uk

ROYAL BALLET

A SEASON IN PICTURES
2018/19

THE ROYAL BALLET SEASON IN PICTURES AND ROYAL BALLET SEASON GENEROUSLY SUPPORTED BY
AUD JEBSEN

Darcey Bussell and Gary Avis in *Façade* © 2019 ROH. Photograph by Andrej Uspenski

THE 2018/19 SEASON

WELCOME TO THE ROYAL BALLET: A SEASON IN PICTURES 2018/19

We are fortunate at The Royal Ballet to have a rich and vital repertory that spans three centuries with an astonishing range of creativity in ballet. Our 2018/19 Season gave audiences at the Royal Opera House, at BP Big Screen events and cinema screenings across the UK, a glimpse of this abundance.

The Season celebrated the traditions of 19th-century ballet and The Royal Ballet's heritage choreographers. The Company also staged revivals of works by Resident Choreographer Wayne McGregor, Artistic Associate Christopher Wheeldon and Artist in Residence Liam Scarlett, as well as the first revival of Crystal Pite's emotive *Flight Pattern*. The 2018/19 Season also saw new works brought to the Main Stage. In November, Alastair Marriott's moving ballet *The Unknown Soldier* commemorated 100 years since the end of World War I and later in the Season it was a great pleasure to welcome Sidi Larbi Cherkaoui to create *Medusa*, his first work for The Royal Ballet. Liam Scarlett created *The Cunning Little Vixen* for The Royal Ballet School, giving the students the opportunity to share the stage with the Company in a mixed programme with Scarlett's *Asphodel Meadows*.

The Linbury Theatre, the West End's newest, most intimate theatre, opened this Season and was host to a wide array of performances. Royal Ballet dancers featured in the inaugural *International Draft Works* and in *New Work, New Music*, presenting exciting new pieces by choreographers including Aletta Collins, Kristen McNally, Goyo Montero, Juliano Nunes, Calvin Richardson and Alexander Whitley.

We ended the Season with a celebration of Margot Fonteyn, our Prima Ballerina Assoluta, who was born 100 years ago this May. Dancers from the Company performed some of the works with which Fonteyn was most famously associated and we were delighted to welcome Darcey Bussell back to the stage to perform as part of a very special evening.

Our Season in summary comprised:

- *Mayerling* (Kenneth MacMillan)
- *La Bayadère* (Natalia Makarova after Marius Petipa)
- *Infra* (Wayne McGregor)
- *The Unknown Soldier* (Alastair Marriott)
- *Symphony in C* (George Balanchine)
- *The Nutcracker* (Peter Wright after Lev Ivanov)
- *Les Patineurs* (Frederick Ashton)
- *Winter Dreams* (Kenneth MacMillan)
- *The Concert* (Jerome Robbins)
- *New Work, New Music* (Linbury Theatre: Aletta Collins, Alexander Whitley, Goyo Montero, Calvin Richardson, Kristen McNally, Juliano Nunes)
- *Asphodel Meadows* (Liam Scarlett)
- *The Two Pigeons* (Frederick Ashton)
- *The Cunning Little Vixen* (Liam Scarlett)
- *Don Quixote* (Carlos Acosta after Marius Petipa)
- *International Draft Works* (Linbury Theatre)
- *Frankenstein* (Liam Scarlett)
- *Romeo and Juliet* (Kenneth MacMillan)
- *Within the Golden Hour* (Christopher Wheeldon)
- *Medusa* (Sidi Larbi Cherkaoui)
- *Flight Pattern* (Crystal Pite)
- *The Firebird* (Mikhail Fokine)
- *A Month in the Country* (Frederick Ashton)
- *Margot Fonteyn: A Celebration*

The Season is recorded here in beautiful photographs of the Company both in performance and in rehearsal. I hope you enjoy this collection and that it may inspire you to see The Royal Ballet in future performances, on both stages of the Royal Opera House or in a cinema near you.

Kevin O'Hare CBE
Director, The Royal Ballet

THE 2018/19 SEASON AT A GLANCE

2018

OCTOBER

MAYERLING
Choreography **Kenneth MacMIllan**
Music **Franz Liszt**
Arranged and orchestrated by **John Lanchbery**
Designer **Nicholas Georgiadis**
Scenario **Gillian Freeman**

Premiere
14 February 1978 (The Royal Ballet)

NOVEMBER

LA BAYADÈRE
Choreography **Natalia Makarova** after **Marius Petipa**
Music **Ludwig Minkus**
Orchestrated by **John Lanchbery**
Production **Natalia Makarova**
Costume designer **Yolanda Sonnabend**
Projection designer **59 Productions**

Premieres
23 January 1877 (Mariinsky Theatre, St Petersburg: choreography by Marius Petipa)
21 May 1980 (American Ballet Theatre)

INFRA/THE UNKNOWN SOLDIER/SYMPHONY IN C

INFRA
Choreography **Wayne McGregor**
Music **Max Richter**
Designer **Julian Opie**
Costume designer **Moritz Junge**

Premiere
13 November 2008 (The Royal Ballet)

THE UNKNOWN SOLDIER
Choreography **Alastair Marriott**
Music **Dario Marianelli**
Costume designer **Jonathan Howells**
Projection designer **Luke Halls**

Premiere
20 November 2018 (The Royal Ballet)

SYMPHONY IN C
Choreography **George Balanchine**
Music **Georges Bizet**
Designer **Anthony Dowell**

Premieres
28 July 1947 (Paris Opera Ballet)
10 July 1950 (revised, New York City Ballet)
20 November 1991 (this production, The Royal Ballet)

DECEMBER-JANUARY

THE NUTCRACKER
Choreography **Peter Wright** after **Lev Ivanov**
Music **Pyotr Il'yich Tchaikovsky**
Original scenario **Marius Petipa**
Production and scenario **Peter Wright**
Designer **Julia Trevelyan Oman**
Production consultant **Roland John Wiley**

Premieres
16 December 1892 (Mariinsky Theatre, St Petersburg)
20 December 1984 (The Royal Ballet, this production)

LES PATINEURS/WINTER DREAMS/THE CONCERT

LES PATINEURS
Choreography **Frederick Ashton**
Music **Giacomo Meyerbeer**
Arranged by **Constant Lambert**
Designer **William Chappell**

Premiere
16 February 1937 (The Vic-Wells Ballet)

WINTER DREAMS
Choreography **Kenneth MacMillan**
Music **Pyotr Il'yich Tchaikovsky**
Arranged by **Phillip Gammon**
Russian Music arrangement **Sarah Freestone**
Designer **Peter Farmer**

Premiere
7 February 1991 (The Royal Ballet)

THE CONCERT
Choreography **Jerome Robbins**
Music **Fryderyk Chopin**
Arranged by **Clare Grundman**
Frontcloth designer **Saul Steinberg**
Costume designer **Irene Sharaff**
Lighting **Jennifer Tipton** and **Les Dickert**

Premiere
6 March 1956 (New York City Ballet)

2019

JANUARY-FEBRUARY

ASPHODEL MEADOWS/THE TWO PIGEONS
ASPHODEL MEADOWS
Choreography **Liam Scarlett**
Music **Francis Poulenc**
Designer **John Macfarlane**
Lighting **Jennifer Tipton**

Premiere
5 May 2010 (The Royal Ballet)

THE TWO PIGEONS
Choreography **Frederick Ashton**
Music **André Messager**
Arranged by **John Lanchbery**
Designer **Jacques Dupont**

Premiere
14 February 1961 (The Royal Ballet)

THE CUNNING LITTLE/VIXEN THE TWO PIGEONS
THE CUNNING LITTLE VIXEN
Choreography **Liam Scarlett**
Music **Leoš Janácek**
Arranged by **Peter Breiner**
Design and concept **Liam Scarlett**
Lighting designer **Les Bone**
Projection designer **Finn Ross**

Premiere
12 Febuary 2019 (The Royal Ballet School)

FEBRUARY

NEW WORK NEW MUSIC:
based on 'a' true story
Choreography **Kristen McNally**
Music **Samantha Fernando**
Costume designer **Adrian Villasenor**

UNCANNY VALLEY
Choreography **Alexander Whitley**
Music **Mica Levi**
Costume designer **Hyemi Shin**

CIRCULAR RUINS
Choreography **Goyo Montero**
Music **Owen Belton**
Costume designer **Fay Fullerton**

TWO SIDES OF
Choreography **Juliano Nunes**
Music **Luke Howard**
Costume designer **Fay Fullerton**

SOMETHING BORROWED
Choreography **Calvin Richardson**
Music **Anna Meredith**
Costume designer **Isabelle Parzygnat**

BLUE MOON
Choreography **Aletta Collins**
Music **David Sawer**
Costume designer **Hyemi Shin**

Premiere of whole programme
6 February 2019 (The Royal Ballet)

MARCH

DON QUIXOTE
Choreography **Carlos Acosta** after **Marius Petipa**
Production **Carlos Acosta**
Original music **Ludwig Minkus**
Arranged and orchestrated by **Martin Yates**
Designer **Tim Hatley**

Premieres
26 December 1869 (Moscow: choreography by Marius Petipa)
30 September 2013 (The Royal Ballet, this production)

FRANKENSTEIN
Choreography **Liam Scarlett**
Music **Lowell Liebermann**
Designer **John Macfarlane**
Projection designer **Finn Ross**

Premiere
4 May 2016 (The Royal Ballet)

ROMEO AND JULIET
Choreography **Kenneth MacMillan**
Music **Sergey Prokofiev**
Designer **Nicholas Georgiadis**

Premiere
9 February 1965 (The Royal Ballet)

APRIL

INTERNATIONAL DRAFT WORKS
INTERCHANGEABLE TEXT
Choreography **Gemma Bond**
Performed by **American Ballet Theater Studio Company**

STEMS
Choreography **Kit Holder**
Performed by **Birmingham Royal Ballet**

SAND and AI
Choreography **Milena Sidorova**
Performed by **Dutch National Ballet**

SEELEN-SPIEL (SOUL GAME)
Choreography **Aleix Martinez**
Performed by **Hamburg Ballet**

JACK
Choreography **Drew Jacoby**
Performed by **Opera Ballet Vlaanderen**

GREY VERSES
Choreography **Brendan Saye**
Performed by **The National Ballet of Canada**

for: jake
Choreography **Douwe Dekkers** and **Samantha Lynch**
Performed by **The Norwegian National Ballet**

ZOHAR
Choreography **Hannah Grennell**
Performed by **The Royal Ballet**

CANTO DE OSSANHA
Choreography **Joshua Junker**
Performed by **The Royal Ballet**

MAY

WITHIN THE GOLDEN HOUR / MEDUSA / FLIGHT PATTERN
WITHIN THE GOLDEN HOUR
Choreography **Christopher Wheeldon**
Music **Ezio Bosso** and **Antonio Vivaldi**
Costume designer **Jasper Conran**

Premiere
22 April 2008 (San Francisco Ballet)

MEDUSA
Choreography **Sidi Larbi Cherkaoui**
Music **Henry Purcell**
Electronic music **Olga Wojciechowska**
Costume director **Olivia Pomp**
Set concept and design **Sidi Larbi Cherkaoui** and **ROH Production**
Associate choreographer **Jason Kittelberger**

Premiere
8 May 2019 (The Royal Ballet)

FLIGHT PATTERN
Choreography **Crystal Pite**
Music **Henryk Mikołaj Górecki**
Costume designer **Nancy Bryant**

Premiere
16 March 2017 (The Royal Ballet)

JUNE

THE FIREBIRD / A MONTH IN THE COUNTRY / SYMPHONY IN C
THE FIREBIRD
Choreography **Mikhail Fokine**
Music **Igor Stravinsky**
Designer **Natalia Goncharova**

Premieres
25 June 1910 (Ballets Russes)
23 August 1954 (Sadler's Wells Ballet, this production)

A MONTH IN THE COUNTRY
Choreography **Frederick Ashton**
Music **Fryderyk Chopin**
Arranged by **John Lanchbery**
Designer **Julia Trevelyan Oman**
Original lighting designer **William Bundy**

Premiere
12 February 1976 (The Royal Ballet)

MARGOT FONTEYN: A CELEBRATION
THE FIREBIRD

THE SLEEPING BEAUTY (Rose Adage)
Choreography **Marius Petipa**
Production **Monica Mason** and **Christopher Newton**
after **Ninette de Valois** and **Nicholas Sergeyev**
Music **Pyotr Il'yich Tchaikovsky**
Original designs **Oliver Messel**
Additional designs **Peter Farmer**

Premieres
3 January 1890 (Mariinsky Theatre, St Petersburg)
15 May 2006 (The Royal Ballet, this production)

NOCTURNE (solo)
Choreography **Frederick Ashton**
Music **Frederick Delius**
Costume designer **Sophie Fedorovitch**

Premiere
10 November 1936 (Vic-Wells Ballet)

THE WISE VIRGINS (solo)
Choreography **Frederick Ashton**
Music **Johann Sebastian Bach**
Orchestrated by **William Walton**
Designer **Rex Whistler**

Premiere
24 April 1940 (Vic-Wells Ballet)

BIRTHDAY OFFERING (variation and pas de deux)
Choreography **Frederick Ashton**
Music **Alexander Konstantinovich Glazunov**
Costume designer **André Levasseur**

Premiere
5 May 1956 (Sadler's Wells Ballet)

ONDINE (Shadow Dance and pas de deux)
Choreography **Frederick Ashton**
Music **Hans Werner Henze**
Costume designer **Lila de Nobili**

Premiere
27 October 1958 (The Royal Ballet)

SYLVIA (from Act I)
Choreography **Frederick Ashton**
Music **Léo Delibes**
Designers **Christopher** and **Robin Ironside**

Premiere
3 September 1952 (Sadler's Wells Ballet)

DAPHNIS AND CHLOË (pas de deux)
Choreography **Frederick Ashton**
Music **Joseph Maurice Ravel**
Costume designer **John Craxton**

Premiere
5 April 1951 (Sadler's Wells Ballet)

ROMEO AND JULIET (Act I pas de deux)

FAÇADE (tango)
Choreography **Frederick Ashton**
Music **William Walton**
Costume designer **John Armstsrong**

Premiere
26 April 1931 (Camargo Society)

LE CORSAIRE (pas de deux)
Choreography **Marius Petipa**
Music **Riccardo Drigo**

Premieres
13 January 1899 (Mariinsky Theatre, St Petersburg)
3 November 1962 (The Royal Ballet, this production)

APPARITIONS (Ballroom Scene)
Choreography **Frederick Ashton**
Music **Franz Liszt**
Designer **Cecil Beaton**

Premiere
11 February 1936 (Sadler's Wells Ballet)

Mayerling

Choreography
Kenneth MacMillan

Photography
Helen Maybanks
© 2018 ROH

Yuhui Choe as Princess Stephanie, Thiago Soares as Crown Prince Rudolf and artists of The Royal Ballet

This page: Melissa Hamilton and Matthew Ball in rehearsal. Rehearsal photography by Andrej Uspenski © 2018 ROH
Opposite page: (clockwise from top left) Lauren Cuthbertson as Mary Vetsera and Thiago Soares as Crown Prince Rudolf; Lara Turk as Empress Elisabeth; Ryoichi Hirano as Crown Prince Rudolf

La Bayadère

Choreography
Natalia Makarova
after Marius Petipa

Photography
Bill Cooper
© 2018 ROH

This page: artists of The Royal Ballet;
Akane Takada as Nikiya
and Steven McRae as Solor

Opposite page: Marianela Nuñez
as Gamzatti

This page: (clockwise from top left) Akane Takada as Nikiya; Calvin Richardson as the Bronze Idol, Yasmine Naghdi as Gamzatti

Opposite page: (clockwise from top left) Matthew Ball in rehearsal; Fumi Kaneko in rehearsal; artists of The Royal Ballet in rehearsal with Natalia Makarova

The Unknown Soldier

Choreography
Alastair Marriott

Photography
Helen Maybanks
© 2018 ROH

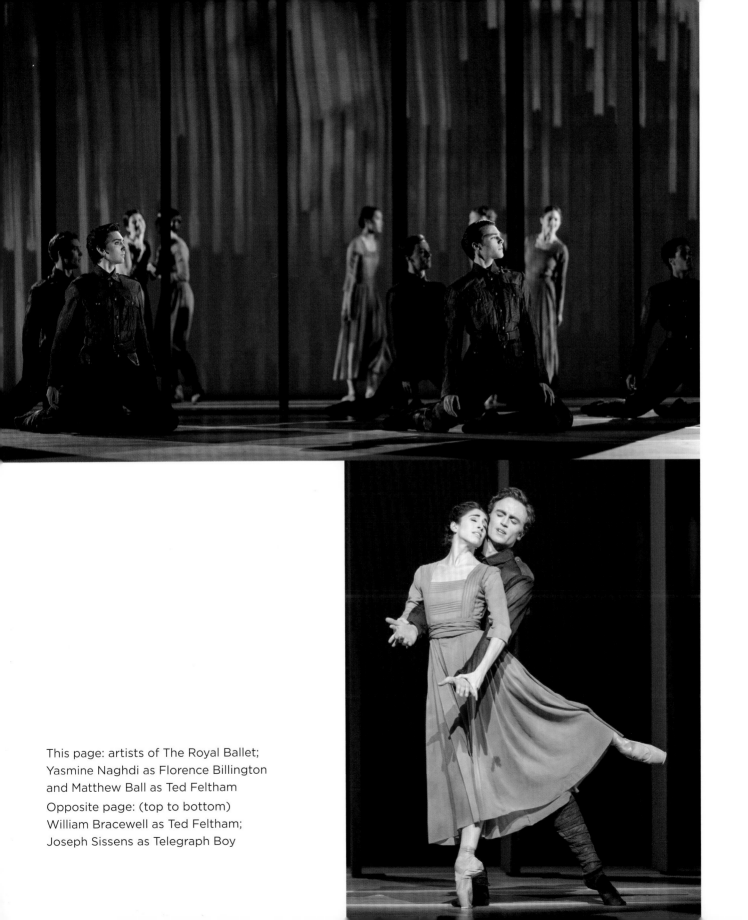

This page: artists of The Royal Ballet;
Yasmine Naghdi as Florence Billington
and Matthew Ball as Ted Feltham
Opposite page: (top to bottom)
William Bracewell as Ted Feltham;
Joseph Sissens as Telegraph Boy

This page: Anna Rose O'Sullivan
and William Bracewell in rehearsal;
Lukas Bjørneboe Brændsrød,
William Bracewell, Stanisław
Węgrzyn and artists of The Royal
Ballet in rehearsal
Opposite page: (top to bottom)
Leo Dixon as Telegraph Boy;
Matthew Ball as Ted Feltham
and Tomas Mock as Harry Patch

This page: artists of The Royal Ballet

Opposite page: (clockwise from top left) William Bracewell and Anna Rose O'Sullivan;
Tristan Dyer and Akane Takada; Marcelino Sambé and Mayara Magri; Matthew Ball and Romany Pajdak

Infra

Choreography
Wayne McGregor

Photography
Helen Maybanks
© 2018 ROH

24

This page: (top to bottom)
Francisco Serrano; Joseph Sissens
Opposite page: (top to bottom) William
Bracewell and Anna Rose O'Sullivan;
Fumi Kaneko and Nicol Edmonds

Symphony in C

Choreography
George Balanchine

Photography
Helen Maybanks
© 2018 ROH

This page: artists of The Royal Ballet

Opposite page: Valentino Zucchetti; Fumi Kaneko

The Nutcracker

Choreography
Peter Wright
after Lev Ivanov

Photography
Alastair Muir
© 2018/2019 ROH

This page: (top to bottom) Itziar Mendizabal and Tomas Mock in the Arabian Dance; Reece Clarke as the Prince and Claire Clavert as the Sugar Plum Fairy

Opposite page: Gary Avis as Herr Drosselmeyer, Marcelino Sambé as Hans-Peter, Fumi Kaneko as the Rose Fairy, Anna Rose O'Sullivan as Clara and artists of The Royal Ballet

This page: (top to bottom) Meaghan Grace Hinkis as Clara and Luca Acri as Hans-Peter; Anna Rose O'Sullivan as Clara with Leo Dixon and Luca Acri in the Chinese Dance

Opposite page: (top to bottom) Anna Rose O'Sullivan as Clara, artists of The Royal Ballet and students of The Royal Ballet School; Marcelino Sambé as Hans-Peter and Alastair Marriott as Herr Drosselmeyer

Les Patineurs

Choreography
Frederick Ashton

Photography
Alice Pennefather
© 2018 ROH

This page: (top to bottom) Melissa Hamilton and Reece Clarke;
Anna Rose O'Sullivan, Marcelino Sambé, Yuhui Choe
Opposite page: (top to bottom) David Yudes; Gina Storm-Jensen and Claire Calvert

This page: artists of The Royal Ballet
Opposite page: (clockwise from top left)
Yuhui Choe in rehearsal; Melissa Hamilton
and Reece Clarke in rehearsal; Mayara
Magri and Gina Storm-Jensen in rehearsal

Winter Dreams

Choreography
Kenneth MacMillan

Photography
Alice Pennefather
© 2018 ROH

This page: (top to bottom)
Vadim Muntagirov as Lt. Colonel
Vershinin and Sarah Lamb as
Masha; Thiago Soares as
Lt. Colonel Vershinin and
Marianela Nuñez as Masha
Opposite page: artists of
The Royal Ballet

This page: (top to bottom) Itziar Mendizabal as Olga and Bennet Gartside as Kulygin; Akane Takada as Irina, Claire Calvert as Olga and Laura Morera as Masha

Opposite page: (clockwise from top left) Laura Morera and Ryoichi Hirano in rehearsal; Sarah Lamb in rehearsal; Sarah Lamb and Vadim Muntagirov in rehearsal

The Concert

Choreography
Jerome Robbins

Photography
Alice Pennefather
© 2018 ROH

This page: (top to bottom)
Sarah Lamb and artists of The Royal Ballet; Lauren Cuthbertson
Opposite page: (top to bottom)
Nicol Edmonds, Beatriz Stix-Brunell and Meaghan Grace Hinkis;
Robert Clark, Lauren Cuthbertson and Kristen McNally

This page: Robert Clark and artists of
The Royal Ballet; Thomas Whitehead
Opposite page: (top to bottom)
Gemma Pitchley-Gale, Romany Pajdak,
Ashley Dean, Leticia Dias, Kristen
McNally and Mayara Magri; Romany
Pajdak, Meaghan Grace Hinkis and
Beatriz Stix-Brunell

New Work
New Music

Choreography
Various

Photography
Alice Pennefather
© 2019 ROH

This page: (top to bottom)
Francisco Serrano and artists
of The Royal Ballet in Calvin
Richardson's *Something
Borrowed*; Joseph Aumeer
and artists of The Royal
Ballet in Alexander
Whitley's *Uncanny Valley*

Opposite page:
(top to bottom) Charlotte
Tonkinson, Mayara Magri,
Mica Bradbury, Fumi
Kaneko, Beatriz Stix-Brunell,
Kristen McNally and Hannah
Grennell in Aletta Collins'
Blue Moon; Chisato Katsura
in Calvin Richardson's
Something Borrowed

This page: (top to bottom) Nadia Mullova-Barley and Harry Churches in Kristen McNally's *based on 'a' true story*; Thiago Soares and Marianela Nuñez in Goyo Montero's *Circular Ruins*

Opposite page: (clockwise from left) Lauren Cuthbertson and Marcelino Sambé in rehearsal; Beatriz Stix-Brunell in rehearsal; Nadia Mullova-Barley in rehearsal

Asphodel Meadows

Choreography
Liam Scarlett

Photography
Bill Cooper
© 2019 ROH

This page: artists of The Royal Ballet
Opposite page: (top to bottom)
Laura Morera and William Bracewell;
Leo Dixon and Sae Maeda

This page: Anna Rose O'Sullivan
and Téo Dubreuil; Laura Morera
and William Bracewell in rehearsal
Opposite page: Fumi Kaneko and
Calvin Richardson; Ryoichi Hirano
and Marianela Nuñez

The Two Pigeons

Choreography
Frederick Ashton

Photography
Bill Cooper and
Tristram Kenton
© 2019 ROH

This page: (top to bottom) Reece Clarke as the Young Man and Beatriz Stix-Brunell as the Young Girl; Lauren Cuthbertson as the Young Girl and Vadim Muntagirov as the Young Man. Photography by Bill Cooper

Opposite page: Yasmine Naghdi as the Young Girl. Photography by Tristram Kenton

This page: Yasmine Naghdi as the Young Girl and Alexander Campbell
as the Young Man. Photography by Tristram Kenton
Opposite page: Lauren Cuthbertson as the Young Girl and Vadim Muntagirov
as the Young Man; Claire Calvert as the Gypsy Girl. Photography by Bill Cooper

The Cunning Little Vixen

Choreography
Liam Scarlett

Photography
Tristram Kenton
© 2019 ROH

This page:
(top to bottom)
Johnny Randall
as Cockerel
and students
of The Royal
Ballet School
as Chickens;
Daichi Ikarashi
as Frog

Opposite page:
(top to bottom)
Madison Bailey
as Sharp-Ears
the Vixen and
Liam Boswell
as Gold-Spur
the Fox;
Liam Boswell
as Gold-Spur
the Fox and
Madison Bailey
as Sharp-Ears
the Vixen

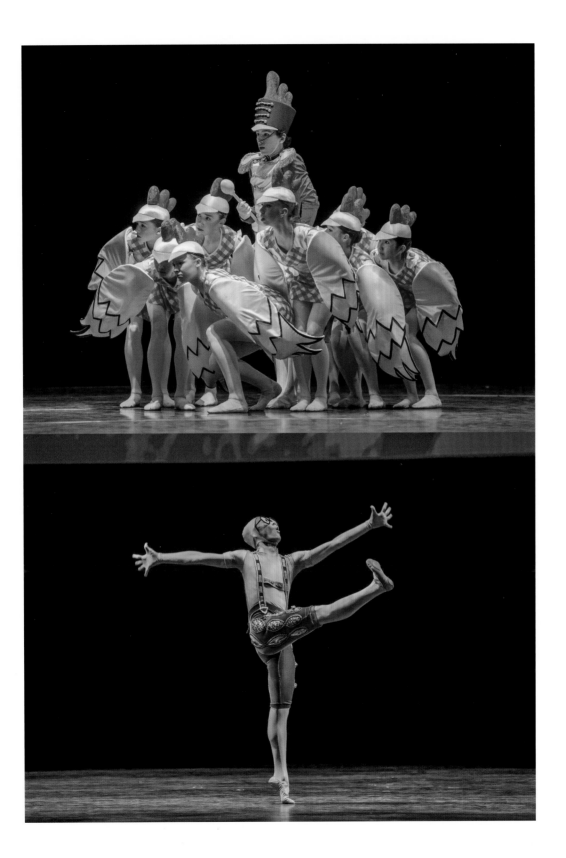

Frankenstein

Choreography
Liam Scarlett

Photography
Bill Cooper
© 2019 ROH

This page: Wei Wang as The Creature; Sarah Lamb as
Elizabeth Lavenza and Ryoichi Hirano as The Creature
Opposite page: Nehemiah Kish as The Creature and
Meaghan Grace Hinkis as Elizabeth Lavenza

This page: Wei Wang as The Creature and Federico Bonelli as Victor Frankenstein
Opposite page: (clockwise from top left) Tristan Dyer as Victor Frankenstein and Sarah Lamb as Elizabeth Lavenza; Nehemiah Kish in rehearsal; Meaghan Grace Hinkis in rehearsal. Rehearsal photography by Andrej Uspenski © 2019 ROH

Don Quixote

Choreography
Carlos Acosta
after Marius Petipa

Photography
Andrej Uspenski
© 2019 ROH

This page: artists of The Royal Ballet
Opposite page: (top to bottom) Valentino
Zucchetti as Espada; Lauren Cuthbertson as
Kitri and Matthew Ball as Basilio

This page: artists of
The Royal Ballet;
Alexander Campbell as
Basilio, Akane Takada
as Kitri and artists of
The Royal Ballet
Opposite page: (top
to bottom) Daniel
Camargo as Basilio
and Fumi Kaneko as
Kitri; Marianela Nuñez
as Kitri

This page: (clockwise from top right) Mayara Magri in rehearsal; Vadim Muntagirov and Natalia Osipova in rehearsal; Marcelino Sambé and Yasmine Naghdi in rehearsal

Opposite page: (clockwise from top left) Akane Takada as Kitri; Yasmine Naghdi as Kitri; Vadim Muntagirov as Basilio; Marcelino Sambé as Basilio

International Draft Works

Choreography
Various

Photography
Bill Cooper
© 2019 ROH

This page: Brandon Lawrence in Kit Holder's *Stems*, Birmingham Royal Ballet; Giovanni Princic and Khayla Fitzpatrick in Milena Sidorova's *Sand*, Dutch National Ballet

Opposite page: (clockwise from top) Artists of the American Ballet Theatre Studio Company in Gemma Bond's *Interchangable Text*, American Ballet Theatre Studio Company; Tiemen Bormans in Drew Jacoby's *Jack*, Opera Ballet Vlaanderen; Kristen McNally and Benjamin Ella in Hannah Grennell's *Zohar*, The Royal Ballet; Chelsy Meiss and Donald Thom in Brendan Saye's *Grey Verses*, The National Ballet of Canada

This page: (top to bottom) Yaiza Coll in Aleix Martinez's *Seelen-Spiel*, Hamburg Ballet; Marc Jubete, Yaiza Coll, Patricia Friza and Nicolas Gläsmann in Aleix Martinez's *Seelen-Spiel*, Hamburg Ballet

Opposite page: (clockwise from top left) Lukas Bjørneboe Brændsrød and Ashley Dean in Joshua Junker's *Canto de Ossanha*, The Royal Ballet; Douwe Dekkers and Samantha Lynch in Douwe Dekkers and Samantha Lynch's *for: jake*, The Norwegian National Ballet; Elena Lobsanova and Nayoa Ebe in Brendan Saye's *Grey Verses*, The National Ballet of Canada; Aya Okumura in Milena Sidorova's *AI*, Dutch National Ballet

Romeo and Juliet

Choreography
Kenneth MacMillan

Photography
Helen Maybanks
© 2019 ROH

73

This page: (top to bottom)
Ryoichi Hirano as Romeo and
Beatriz Stix-Brunell as Juliet;
Christopher Saunders as Lord
Capulet and Christina Arestis
as Lady Capulet

Opposite page: (clockwise from
top left) Helen Crawford as Nurse
and Beatriz Stix-Brunell as Juliet;
Cesar Corrales as Romeo and
Francesca Hayward as Juliet;
Marcelino Sambé as Romeo and
Anna Rose O'Sullivan as Juliet;
Lauren Cuthbertson as Juliet
and Matthew Ball as Romeo

This page: (clockwise from top left)
Marcelino Sambé and Anna Rose O'Sullivan in rehearsal;
Anna Rose O'Sullivan and Marcelino Sambé in rehearsal;
Ryoichi Hirano and Beatriz Stix-Brunell in rehearsal
Opposite page: (top to bottom) Beatriz Stix-Brunell as Juliet
and Ryoichi Hirano as Romeo; Natalia Osipova as Juliet

This page: Leo Dixon; Sarah Lamb
and Alexander Campbell

Opposite page: (top to bottom)
Sarah Lamb, Alexander Campbell,
Francesca Hayward and Valentino
Zucchetti in rehearsal; Yuhui Choe
and James Hay in rehearsal

Within the
Golden Hour

Choreography
Christopher Wheeldon

Photography
Tristram Kenton
© 2019 ROH

Medusa

Choreography
Sidi Larbi Cherkaoui

Photography
Tristram Kenton
© 2019 ROH

This page: (top to bottom) Matthew Ball
as Perseus, Natalia Osipova as Medusa and
artists of The Royal Ballet as Soldiers;
Natalia Osipova as Medusa
Opposite page: Natalia Osipova as Medusa
and artists of The Royal Ballet as Soldiers

This page: Ryoichi Hirano as Poseidon and Natalia Osipova as Medusa; Natalia Osipova and Olivia Cowley in rehearsal
Opposite page: (left to right) Mica Bradbury as a Priestess; Natalia Osipova as Medusa and Ryoichi Hirano as Poseidon

Flight Pattern

Choreography
Crystal Pite

Photography
Tristram Kenton
© 2019 ROH

This page: artists of The Royal Ballet
Opposite page: artists of The Royal Ballet

84

This page: Kristen McNally and artists of The Royal Ballet

Opposite page: (top to bottom) Isabella Gasparini, Romany Pajdak
and artists of The Royal Ballet; artists of The Royal Ballet

The Firebird

Choreography
Mikhail Fokine

Photography
Tristram Kenton
© 2019 ROH

This page: (clockwise from top right) Edward Watson as Ivan Tsarevich and Yasmine Naghdi as The Firebird; Ryoichi Hirano as Ivan Tsarevich and Mayara Magri as The Firebird; Itziar Mendizabal as The Firebird

Opposite page: Helen Crawford as Tsarevna, Ryoichi Hirano as Ivan Tsarevich, artists of The Royal Ballet and students of The Royal Ballet School

This page: (top to bottom) Ryoichi Hirano as Ivan Tsarevich and artists of The Royal Ballet; Christina Arestis as Tsarevna and artists of The Royal Ballet

Opposite page: (clockwise from top left) Yasmine Naghdi and Edward Watson in rehearsal, Ryoichi Hirano and Mayara Magri in rehearsal; Itziar Mendizabal and Nehemiah Kish in rehearsal

A Month in the Country

Choreography
Frederick Ashton

Photography
Tristram Kenton
© 2019 ROH

This page: (top to bottom) David Yudes as Kolia; Marianela Nuñez as Natalia Petrovna

Opposite page: (top to bottom) James Hay as Kolia and Francesca Hayward as Vera; Lauren Cuthbertson as Natalia Petrovna and Vadim Muntagirov as Beliaev

This page: Gary Avis and Marianela Nuñez in rehearsal; Vadim Muntagirov in rehearsal

Opposite page: Marianela Nuñez as Natalia Petrovna

Symphony in C

Choreography
George Balanchine

Photography
Tristram Kenton
© 2019 ROH

This page: artists of The Royal Ballet
Opposite page: (top to bottom) artists of
The Royal Ballet; David Donnelly, Melissa
Hamilton, Olivia Cowley and Tomas Mock

Margot Fonteyn: A Celebration

Choreography
Various

Photography
Andrej Uspenski
© 2019 ROH

This page: (top to bottom) David Hallberg and Natalia Osipova in *Romeo and Juliet*; Romany Pajdak in *The Wise Virgins*

Opposite page: (clockwise from top left) Alexander Campbell and Anna Rose O'Sullivan in *Daphnis and Chloë*; Francesca Hayward in *Ondine*; Lauren Cuthbertson and Matthew Ball in *Apparitions*; Beatriz Stix-Brunell in *Nocturne*

This page: (top to bottom) Vadim Muntagirov and Yasmine Naghdi in *Le Corsaire*; Marianela Nuñez in *The Sleeping Beauty*
Opposite page: Fumi Kaneko in *Birthday Offering*; Ryoichi Hirano and Sarah Lamb in *Birthday Offering*

ARTISTS AND STAFF OF THE ROYAL BALLET 2018/19

Top, left to right:
Royal Ballet Director Kevin O'Hare, Royal Ballet Music Director Koen Kessels, Resident Choreographer Wayne McGregor, Artistic Associate Christopher Wheeldon and Artist in Residence Liam Scarlett

Bottom, left to right:
Administrative Director Heather Baxter, Clinical Director Gregory Retter and Rehearsal Director Christopher Saunders

PRINCIPALS
Left to right:
Matthew Ball
Federico Bonelli
Alexander Campbell

Lauren
Cuthbertson
Francesca Hayward
Ryoichi Hirano

Nehemiah Kish
Sarah Lamb
Steven McRae

Laura Morera
Vadim Muntagirov
Yasmine Naghdi

103

Marianela Nuñez
Natalia Osipova
Thiago Soares

Akane Takada
Edward Watson

PRINCIPAL CHARACTER ARTISTS
Left to right:
Christina Arestis
Gary Avis
Bennet Gartside
Alastair Marriott
Elizabeth McGorian

Kristen McNally
Christopher Saunders
Thomas Whitehead

CHARACTER ARTISTS
Left to right:
Jonathan Howells
Philip Mosley

FIRST SOLOISTS
Left to right:
William Bracewell
Claire Calvert
Yuhui Choe
Cesar Corrales
Helen Crawford

Melissa Hamilton
James Hay
Tierney Heap
Fumi Kaneko
Hikaru Kobayashi

Mayara Magri
Itziar Mendizabal
Marcelino Sambé
Beatriz Stix-Brunell
Valentino Zucchetti

SOLOISTS
Left to right:
Luca Acri
Reece Clarke
Olivia Cowley
Tristan Dyer
Nicol Edmonds

105

Benjamin Ella

Elizabeth Harrod

Meaghan Grace
Hinkis

Paul Kay

Emma Maguire

Fernando Montaño

Anna Rose
O'Sullivan

Calvin Richardson

FIRST ARTISTS
Left to right:

Tara-Brigitte
Bhavnani

Camille Bracher

David Donnelly

Téo Dubreuil

Kevin Emerton

Isabella Gasparini

Hannah Grennell

Nathalie Harrison

Tomas Mock

Erico Montes

Romany Pajdak

Demelza Parish

Gemma Pitchley-Gale

Joseph Sissens

Leticia Stock

Gina Storm-Jensen

Lara Turk

David Yudes

ARTISTS

Left to right:

Sophie Allnatt

Joseph Aumeer

Lukas Bjørneboe Brændsrød

Grace Blundell

Mica Bradbury

Annette Buvoli

Harry Churches

  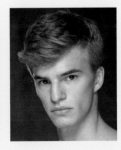  

Ashley Dean

Leticia Dias

Leo Dixon

Joonhyuk Jun

Joshua Junker

Chisato Katsura
Isabel Lubach
Sae Maeda
Nadia Mullova-
Barley
Aiden O'Brien

Julia Roscoe
Giacomo Rovero
Mariko Sasaki
Francisco Serrano
Charlotte Tonkinson

Stanisław Węgrzyn

**AUD JEBSEN
YOUNG DANCERS**
Left to right:
Lania Atkins
Harris Bell
Harrison Lee
Taisuke Nakao

Katharina Nikelski
Amelia Palmiero
Amelia Townsend
Yu Hang

**PRIX DE
LAUSANNE
DANCER**

Davide Loricchio

**ROYAL BALLET
STAFF**

Left to right:
Ballet Masters
Gary Avis
Ricardo Cervera
Jonathan Howells
Ballet Mistress
Samantha Raine
**Assistant Ballet
Mistress**
Sian Murphy

**Senior Teacher and
Répétiteur to the
Principal Artists**
Alexander Agadzhanov
Répétiteurs
Lesley Collier
Jonathan Cope
**Guest Principal
Ballet Master**
Christopher Carr
**Principal Guest
Répétiteur**
Carlos Acosta

**Principal Guest
Teacher**
Elizabeth Anderton
Olga Evreinoff
**Senior Benesh
Choreologist**
Anna Trevien
Benesh Choreologists
Gregory Mislin
Lorraine Gregory

Principal Guest Conductor
Barry Wordsworth
Head of Music Staff
Robert Clark
**Learning and Participation
Creative Associate (Ballet)**
David Pickering
**Ballet Rehabilitation
Specialist and
Class Teacher**
Brian Maloney
**Artistic Scheduling
Manager**
Philip Mosley

**Company and
Tour Manager**
Rachel Vickers
Creative Producer
Emma Southworth
Artistic Administrator
Rachel Hollings
Stage Manager
Johanna Adams Farley
Head of Ballet Press
Ashley Woodfield

Aud Jebsen with dancers of the Aud Jebsen Young Dancers Programme past and present: (left to right) Sae Maeda, Grace Blundell, Harrison Lee, Taisuke Nakao, Harris Bell, Charlotte Tonkinson, Yu Hang, Joonhyuk Jun, Julia Roscoe, Katharina Nikelski, Ashley Dean, Giacomo Rovero, Aud Jebsen, Leo Dixon, Amelia Townsend, Harry Churches, Nadia Mullova-Barley, Aiden O'Brien, Isabel Lubach, Lukas Bjørneboe Brændsrød

The Royal Ballet

Patron **HM The Queen**
President **HRH The Prince of Wales**
Vice-President **The Lady Sarah Chatto**

Director† **Kevin O'Hare CBE**

Music Director **Koen Kessels**
Resident Choreographer‡ **Wayne McGregor CBE**
Artistic Associate†† **Christopher Wheeldon OBE**

†Position generously supported by Lady Ashcroft
‡Position generously supported by Linda and Philip Harley
††Position generously supported by Kenneth and Susan Green

Principals

Matthew Ball
Federico Bonelli
Alexander Campbell
Lauren Cuthbertson
David Hallberg*
Francesca Hayward
Ryoichi Hirano
Nehemiah Kish
Sarah Lamb
Steven McRae
Laura Morera
Vadim Muntagirov
Yasmine Naghdi
Marianela Nuñez
Natalia Osipova
Thiago Soares
Akane Takada
Edward Watson

Principal Character Artists

Christina Arestis
Gary Avis
Bennet Gartside
Alastair Marriott
Elizabeth McGorian
Kristen McNally
Christopher Saunders
Thomas Whitehead

First Soloists

William Bracewell
Claire Calvert
Yuhui Choe
Cesar Corrales
Helen Crawford
Melissa Hamilton
James Hay
Tierney Heap
Fumi Kaneko
Hikaru Kobayashi
Mayara Magri
Itziar Mendizabal
Marcelino Sambé
Beatriz Stix-Brunell
Valentino Zucchetti

Soloists

Luca Acri
Reece Clarke
Olivia Cowley
Tristan Dyer
Nicol Edmonds
Benjamin Ella
Elizabeth Harrod
Meaghan Grace Hinkis
Paul Kay
Emma Maguire
Fernando Montaño
Anna Rose O'Sullivan
Calvin Richardson

First Artists

Tara-Brigitte Bhavnani
Camille Bracher
David Donnelly
Téo Dubreuil
Kevin Emerton
Isabella Gasparini
Hannah Grennell
Nathalie Harrison
Tomas Mock
Erico Montes
Romany Pajdak
Demelza Parish
Gemma Pitchley-Gale
Joseph Sissens
Leticia Stock
Gina Storm-Jensen
Lara Turk
David Yudes

Artists

Sophie Allnatt
Joseph Aumeer
Lukas Bjørneboe Brændsrød
Grace Blundell
Mica Bradbury
Annette Buvoli
Harry Churches
Ashley Dean
Leticia Dias
Leo Dixon
Joonhyuk Jun
Joshua Junker
Chisato Katsura
Isabel Lubach
Sae Maeda
Nadia Mullova-Barley
Aiden O'Brien
Julia Roscoe
Giacomo Rovero
Mariko Sasaki
Francisco Serrano
Charlotte Tonkinson
Stanisław Węgrzyn

Aud Jebsen Young Dancers Programme

Lania Atkins
Harris Bell
Harrison Lee
Taisuke Nakao
Katharina Nikelski
Amelia Palmiero
Amelia Townsend
Yu Hang

Prix de Lausanne dancer
Davide Loricchio

*Guest Artist

§ Position generously
supported by Ricki Gail
and Robert Conway

Rehearsal Director
Christopher Saunders

Ballet Masters
Gary Avis
Ricardo Cervera

*Ballet Master
and Character Artist*
Jonathan Howells

Ballet Mistress
Samantha Raine

Assistant Ballet Mistress
Sian Murphy

*Senior Teacher and
Répétiteur to the
Principal Artists*
Alexander Agadzhanov

Répétiteurs
Lesley Collier
Jonathan Cope

Senior Benesh Choreologist
Anna Trevien

Benesh Choreologists
Gregory Mislin
Lorraine Gregory
Melanie Simpkin
(Maternity cover)

*Learning and Participation
Creative Associate (Ballet)*
David Pickering

Artist in Residence
Liam Scarlett

Head of Music Staff
Robert Clark

Music Staff
Philip Cornfield
Craig Edwards
Michael Pansters
Tim Qualtrough
Kate Shipway
Paul Stobart

Music Administrator
Nigel Bates

Creative Producer
Emma Southworth

Senior Producer
Amanda Skoog

Producer
Hannah Mayhew

Assistant to the Producers
Adrienne Miller

Video Archive Manager
Bennet Gartside

Administrative Director
Heather Baxter

Company and Tour Manager
Rachel Vickers

*Artistic Scheduling Manager
and Character Artist*
Philip Mosley

Artistic Administrator
Rachel Hollings

Financial Controller
Cathy Helweg

Deputy Company Manager
Elizabeth Ferguson

*Assistant Producer
(Main Stage)*
Rhiannon Savell

Assistant to the Director
Lettie Heywood

Administrative Co-ordinator
Yvonne Hunte

Management Accountant
Orsola Ricciardelli

Contracts Administrator
Sarah Quarman-Rose

Clinical Director, Ballet Healthcare
Gregory Retter

Clinical Lead
Richard Clark

Chartered Physiotherapists
Gemma Hilton
Moira McCormack
Robin Vellosa

Pilates Instructor
Jane Paris

Gyrotonic Instructor
Fiona Kleckham

Occupational Psychologist
Britt Tajet-Foxell

*Ballet Rehabilitation
Specialist and Class Teacher*
Brian Maloney

Ballet Rehabilitation Coach
Ursula Hageli

Ballet Masseurs
Tatina Semprini
Konrad Simpson
Helen Wellington

Sports Science
Austin Flood
Adam Mattiussi
Gregor Rosenkranz

Registered Dietician
Jacqueline Birtwisle

Medical Advisor
Kate Hutchings

Company Podiatrist
Denzil Trebilcock

Healthcare Co-ordinator
Sally Peerless

Guest Principal Ballet Master
Christopher Carr

Principal Guest Répétiteur
Carlos Acosta

Principal Guest Teachers
Elizabeth Anderton
Olga Evreinoff

Guest Teachers
Boris Akimov
Jacquelin Barrett
Yannick Boquin
Darcey Bussell
Deirdre Chapman
Felipe Diaz
Johnny Eliasen
Valeri Hristov
Andrey Klemm
David Makhateli
Laurent Novis
Meelis Pakri
Alejandro Parente
Alessandra Pasquali
François Petit
Stephane Phavorin
Roland Price
Matz Skoog
Paola Vismara

Principal Guest Conductor
Barry Wordsworth

Conductors
Andrew Griffiths
Boris Gruzin
Jonathan Lo
Paul Murphy
Emmanuel Plasson
Pavel Sorokin
Martin Yates

Constant Lambert Conducting Fellow
Thomas Jung

Governors of the Royal Ballet Companies

Chairman
Dame Jenny Abramsky DBE

Sir Matthew Bourne OBE
Hilary S Carty BMA CCMI
The Lady Deighton
Stephen Jefferies
Jeanetta Laurence OBE
Sir David Normington GCB
Christopher Nourse
Derek Purnell
Ian Taylor
The Duchess of
    Wellington OBE
Monica Zamora

Honorary Secretary
Peter Wilson